Bradwell'[s]

ECLECTICA
EDINBURGH

Published by Bradwell Books
9 Orgreave Close Sheffield S13 9NP
Email: books@bradwellbooks.co.uk

1st Edition

ISBN: 9781909914186

Print: Gutenberg Press, Malta

Design and artwork by: Andrew Caffrey

Photograph Credits: Shutterstock and
Mercat Tours credited individually.
All other images ©Fiona Dalhousie.

Bibliography

www.executedtoday.com
www.festivalsedinburgh.com
www.glasgowguide.co.uk
www.mcvities.co.uk
www.onlyinedinburgh.com
www.scotland.gov.uk
www.scottishbrewing.com
www.visitscotland.com

CAMPBELL, DONALD, Edinburgh: A Cultural
and Literary History (Cities of the Imagination),
Signal Books, 2003

HOLLAND, RICHARD, Scottish Ghost Stories,
Bradwell Books, 2013

JONES, RICHARD, History and Mystery Walks
of Edinburgh, AA Publishing, 2009

Acknowledgements:

I would like to thank everyone who shared
their favourite parts of Edinburgh with me and
especially the helpful staff at the People's Museum
in Canongate. A special thank you to Victoria from
Mercat Tours for kindly giving permission for their
photographs to be included in this book and to
Taste of Scotland on North Bridge for allowing
photographs to be taken on their premises. I would
also like to thank the passers-by who stopped and
volunteered the history of closes, allowed their hand
to be photographed rubbing Bobby's nose and the
lady who was walking her dog who told me about
Queen Street Gardens and let me have a peek
inside – she really made my day.

Bradwell's
ECLECTICA
EDINBURGH

Fiona Dalhousie

BRADWELL
BOOKS

Contents

INTRODUCTION

Edinburgh, the capital city of Scotland, is dominated by its castle and is a place of contrasts with the narrow closes of the Old Town and the Georgian houses of the not so New Town.

HUMOUR

The people of Edinburgh are renowned for their great sense of humour, so here is a collection of rib-tickling jokes from the heartland of Scotland.

MURDERS

Burke and Hare selling murder victims' bodies, a half-hanged woman who springs back to life, murdered children and bodies under the car park; just a few of the unsavoury goings on in Auld Reekie.

LOCAL DIALECT

Learn a few words that might be of use during a visit to Auld Reekie. Find out the difference between clap and clapshot, a lug and a lum, and Hogmanay and Ne'erday.

SCOTTISH RECIPES

Try these Scottish recipes for cock-a-leekie soup, kedgeree and petticoat tails. There is no recipe for haggis here but a good place to buy some is in the Taste of Scotland shop on North Bridge.

CLANS AND TARTANS

King George II banned the wearing of Highland dress with severe penalties for those who disobeyed. In 1822, Sir Walter Scott encouraged the wearing of tartan for King George IV's visit to Edinburgh.

WALKS

Walk in the Old Town and discover the Elephant Café, Greyfriars Bobby and Deacon Brodie's haunts. The New Town walk explores the buildings and places where famous people once lived.

LOCAL CUSTOMS

Edinburgh is a great place for celebrations, whether it be Hogmanay with its amazing fireworks and the emotional singing of 'Auld Lang Syne', Burns Night and a few toasts or the Edinburgh Festival and the Fringe.

LOCAL HISTORY

The doukin' of witches in the Nor' Loch, now Princes Street Gardens, the brewing of beer, banking, digestive biscuits and fishwives selling herring all played a part in the fortunes of Edinburgh.

GHOST STORIES

Auld Reekie is full of ghost stories and strange happenings in the Old Town around the Royal Mile and South Bridge. Many witches were burnt at the stake near Edinburgh Castle.

LOCAL SPORTS

This is where golf was so popular that it had to be banned by Act of Parliament in 1457 as it was interfering with essential archery practice. In the 1600s James Patterson built a tenement he called Golfer's Land with his winnings.

FAMOUS LOCALS

It was hard to choose just a few famous people from Edinburgh as there are so many that could have been mentioned: writers, scientists, philosophers, engineers, economists etc.

INTRODUCTION

EDINBURGH, SCOTLAND'S CAPITAL CITY, HAS A COSMOPOLITAN FEEL WITH NEARLY **ONE AND A HALF MILLION** OVERSEAS VISITORS ENJOYING THE CITY **EVERY YEAR**

The National Museum of Scotland is the most popular attraction in the United Kingdom outside London, and Edinburgh Castle, with well over a million visitors a year, is Scotland's most popular paid-for visitor attraction. The Royal International Tattoo, with its massed pipes and drums, is held on Edinburgh Castle's floodlight esplanade and is a stunning spectacle. The Edinburgh International Festival and the Fringe attract over two and a half million visitors every year and over 300,000 come

Victoria Street leading down to the Grassmarket

especially for the Edinburgh Book Festival. Always a place for a good shindig, Edinburgh excels in its celebrations of Hogmanay and Ne'erday.

You might say that arriving at Edinburgh's main railway station is a novel experience as it is named after Sir Walter Scott's Waverley series of novels. There are two main exits from the station and they take you to what may seem like two different cities. The Market Street exit immediately confronts you with hills and stairs – lots of stairs and narrow passageways called closes that run between the buildings as you walk through the Old Town. The Princes Street exit takes you onto a wide, airy street and turning left you will see the Scott Monument in Princes Street Gardens and the iconic Jenners department store building on the corner of St David Street. This is the New Town with its Georgian architecture, but the character of the Old Town is forever present as it rises high above the far side of Princes Street Gardens. Edinburgh Castle, sitting proud on Castle Rock, somehow connects the Old with the New. It is a castle that is not only seen but heard, as each day, except Sundays, the One O'Clock Gun is fired and its roar reverberates around the city.

The Old Town is steeped in history with the Royal Mile running from the Castle, where there has been a stronghold since the time of Edwin of Deira, who died in 633, all the way to the modern Scottish Parliament building designed by Catalan architect Enric Miralles (1955–2000). Edwin's Fort became known as Din-Eidyn and later as Edwinesburch and it is easy to see how it changed to the more easily pronounced Edinburgh. The Royal Mile is really four streets – Castlehill, Lawnmarket, High Street and Canongate – and was described by Daniel Defoe in 1723 as 'the largest, longest and finest street for Buildings and Number of Inhabitants, not only in Britain, but in the World…' Victoria Street curves down from the George IV Bridge to the Grassmarket and is a reminder of times past. Cowgate runs under the George IV Bridge and South Bridge to St Mary's Street. Robert Louis Stevenson said, in 1878, 'To look over the South Bridge and see the Cowgate below full of crying hawkers, is to view one rank of society from the other in the twinkling of an eye.' There is a plaque with Stevenson's observations on a building in Cowgate that also has the

Cowgate and the TOON COOcillor

hind end of a cow sticking out of the wall with a caption 'The TOON COOcillor'! This medieval Old Town is certainly full of character and history, a place of closes and courts, nooks and crannies – and perhaps even ghosts.

Charlotte Square

The New Town, on the other hand, has wider streets set out in an organised grid system, Georgian architecture, and large private gardens owned by groups of residents. Charlotte Square, designed by Robert Adam, has been described as one of the most beautiful squares in Europe. Number 7, the Georgian House, is owned by the National Trust for Scotland so you can visit and explore the joys of living in these grand houses. The Royal Botanic Garden Edinburgh used to be where Waverely Station now stands but has been at Inverleith since 1820. This is the area where the wealthy New Town Georgians built their summer villas, and in the Botanic Gardens stands Inverleith House, built for James Rocheid in 1774, a good example of the grandeur of these residences.

Uncontained Arts publicise their show, Treasure Island, during the Edinburgh Fringe Festival SHUTTERSTOCK/STEPHEN FINN

Eclectica is just a flavour of Edinburgh, perhaps the beginnings of a love affair with this international city or a reminder of well-worn streets and half-forgotten memories. Whether you are an Edinburgh resident or a visitor there is always something new to see, a bit more history to investigate, festivals, celebrations and just the enjoyment of walking round this city of contrasts.

FIONA DALHOUSIE

LOCAL DIALECT

LEARN A FEW WORDS THAT MIGHT BE OF USE DURING A VISIT TO **AULD REEKIE**.

FIND OUT THE DIFFERENCE BETWEEN **CLAP** AND **CLAPSHOT**, **A LUG** AND **A LUM**, AND **HOGMANAY** AND **NE'ERDAY**.

A

Auld Clootie – the devil
Auld Reekie (or Reikie) – Edinburgh

B

Bairn – child
Bawbee – old halfpenny
Beastie – insect
Blether – chat, natter
Boggin' – horrible, very dirty, smelly
Brae – hill
Braw – fine, lovely
Breeks – trousers
Broth – thick soup

C

Cannae – cannot
Champit – mashed
Clap – stroke an animal, pat
Clapshot – tatties and neeps mashed together
Close – passageway or lane
Clype – tell-tale

D

Deek – look
Dingie – dull
Dinnae – don't
Deochandorus – a drink before leaving

Dreich – dull, miserable weather

Dowt – cigarette end

F

Flech – flea

Flit – move house

Firth – estuary

Foosty – mouldy, stale

Forkietail – earwig

G

Galluses – trouser braces

Guid – good

Glaur –sticky, mud

Gloamin' – twilight, dusk

Greet – cry, weep

H

Havering – talking nonsense

Hessy – hide and seek

Hogmanay – New Year's Eve

Hoose – house

How no? – why not?

J

Jag – injection, sharp prick

Jiggered – exhausted, worn out

K

Ken – know

Kirk – church

L

Land – tenement

Luckenbooth – shop front

Lug – ear

Lum – chimney

M

Mercat – market

Mind – remember

Muckle – very big

N

Nae – no, not

Naebother – no trouble

Ne'erday – New Year's Day

Nicht – night
Noo – now

O

Oose – fluff, dust

P

Peely-wally – pale and sickly looking
Pinnie – apron
Peevers – hopscotch
Piece – sandwich

S

Sair – sore
Scullery – kitchen
Scunner – feel disgust, dislike
Selkie – seal
Shed – parting in hair
Smout – small person or child
Spurtle – wooden spoon
Stookie – plaster cast
Stoorie – dusty
Swither – undecided which to choose
Sybies – spring onions

Syver – drain, street gutter

T

Tatties – potatoes
Toon – town
Twa – two

W

Wait on –wait for
Wee – small
Weegie – Glaswegian
Wheesht – be quiet
Windae – window

Y

Yin – one

Robert Fergusson was born near North Bridge and sadly he fell down some stairs and as a result was sent to Bedlam, where he died. His tombstone and epitaph in Canongate Kirkyard were paid for by another poet, **Rabbie Burns.**

AULD REIKIE
by ROBERT FERGUSSON *(1750–74)*

Auld Reikie means old and smoky and it is still used in an affectionate manner to describe Edinburgh.

Here are a few lines from this long poem which describes everyday life in the toon in the mid-1700s.

Gillespie's[1] snuff should prime the nose

O' her that to the market[2] goes,

If she wad like to shun the smells

That float around frae market cells;

Where wames o' painches sav'ry scent

To nostrils gie great discontent.

Now wha in Albion could expect

O' cleanliness sic great neglect?

Nae Hottentot that daily lairs,

Mang tripe, and ither clarty wares,

Hath ever yet conceived or seen,

Beyond the Line, sic scenes unclean.

Despite his complaints about smells and cleanliness, he goes on to say:

Reikie, fareweel! I ne'er could part
Wi' thee, but wi' a dowie heart.

[1] The Gillespie brothers were tobacconists in Edinburgh and very wealthy.

[2] There was a vegetable market in the High Street between the Tron Church and St. Giles'.

RASHIE COAT

a traditional Scottish fairy tale

Rashie Coat wis a king's dochter, an' her father wanted her tae be married but she didna like the man. Her father said she had to tak him an' she didna ken whit tae dae. Sae she gaed awa tae the hen-wife. The hen-wife said: 'Say ye willna tak him unless they gie ye a coat o' beaten gowd.' They gied her a coat o' beaten gowd but she still didna want him. Sae she went tae the hen-wife again, who said: 'Say ye winna tak him unless they gie ye a coat made o' the feathers o' aw the birds.' Sae the king sent a man wi a great heap o' corn tae feed the birds and collect their feathers tae make a coat but she still didna want him. She gaed tae the hen-wife again who said: 'Say ye winna tak him unless they gie ye a coat o' rashes an' a pair o slippers.' They gied her a coat o' rashes an a pair o' slippers but she still didna want tae tak him an' the hen-wife said she couldna help her ony mair.

She left her father's hoose and gaed faur until she came to a king's hoose. She said she wis seeking service an' they set her in tae the kitchen tae wash the dishes. On the Sabbath day, they went tae the kirk, an' left her at hame tae cook the dinner. A fairy telt her tae gang, an' put on her coat o' beaten gowd an' gang tae the kirk. Sae Rashie Coat pit on her coat o' beaten gowd and gaed tae the kirk.

The king's son fell in luv wi her but she cam hame afore the kirk finished and she found the dinner cooked, and naebody kent she had been oot.

The next Sabbath, the fairy came again, and telt her tae pit on the coat o' feathers and gang tae the kirk. She pit on the coat o' feathers, an' gaed tae the kirk. She cam oot afore it finished and she went hame an' found the dinner cooked, an' naebody kent she had been oot.

The next Sabbath, the fairy came tae her again, an' telt her tae pit on the coat o' rashes an' the pair o' slippers an' gang tae the kirk again. She did it aw an' this time the king's son sat near the door, an' when he seen Rashie Coat slippin' oot, he slipped oot an' aw and gripped her. She gat awa frae him an' ran hame but she lost ane o' her slippers an' he took it up. He declared he wad marry onyone who could get the slipper on. Sae aw the leddies tried tae get the slipper on an' it wadna fit nane o' them. The auld hen-wife's dochter nippit her fit an' she clippit her fit an' gat it on sae the king's son wis gaun tae marry her. He wis ridin on a horse an' her ahint him an' they came tae a wood and a bird sittin' on a tree said:

> *Nippit fit and clippit fit*
> *Ahint the king's son rides*
> *But bonny fit and pretty fit*
> *Ahint the caudron hides.*

When the king's son heard this, he flang aff the hen-wife's dochter, an' came hame again, an leukit inside the caudron, an' there he found Rashie Coat greetin' for her slipper. He tried her fit wi' the slipper, an' it gaed on fine. Sae he married her and they lived happily ever efter.

A COLLECTION OF RIB-TICKLING JOKES FROM EDINBURGH

MAGGIE: Ma wee sister his jist flitted tae Morningside and I've heard it is sae posh there that they divvnae even have sex.

AGNES: Yir no right, yi know. Ah know fur a fact that they still have their coal delivered in sex.

Tourist: *OMG, what an awesome bridge! Do you know what it's called?*

Local: *Aye, Ah dae. It's the Forth Road Bridge*

Tourist: *Gee, what happened to the other three?*

There is a fair amount of rivalry between Edinburgh and Glasgow and Edinburgh folk tend to call Glaswegians Weegies.

Near Waverley Station there was a kiosk selling raffle tickets and it is said that the prizes were:

1st prize:
One week's holiday in Madrid

2nd prize:
One week's holiday in Glasgow

3rd prize:
Two weeks' holiday in Glasgow!

Donald went tae visit a psychiatrist in Edinburgh, no far frae Princes Street.

The psychiatrist asked him what had brought him here.

Donald said, 'Weel, it's like this. Ah think Ah'm a dug and a dinnae ken whit tae dae aboot it.'

The Psychiatrist said, 'Just lie down here on the couch and tell me all about it.'

Donald said, 'Ah cannae dae that. Ah'm no allowed on the furniture!'

....

Carol: Hi, Katy, how wis yir night oot wi Malky?

Katy: It wis OK. We went tae the pub and then we went back tae his place.

Carol: Wis it just OK, then?

Katy: Aye, we watched three DVDs back tae back but unfortunately Ah wasnae facing the telly!

Ma wife Maggie had five sisters and she wis the last o' them tae get married.

We had a great weddin' but the confetti wis awfy dirty!

....

Mrs MacIver went tae the offices of the Scotsman to put her husband's death in the paper.

She asked how much it would be and the girl behind the desk said, 'The cheapest is a fiver but you'll not get many words for that. Write down on this bit of paper what you want to say.'

Mrs MacIver wrote, George MacIver of Leith is dead. The girl said, 'You can have a few more words than that.'

Mrs MacIver took back the bit of paper and wrote, George MacIver is dead. Ford van for sale.

Two Weegies were visiting Edinburgh for the day when they saw a notice in a shop window that said 'Suits £5, Shirts £2, Trousers £2.50'. Jimmy thought that this was a right good bargain and they worked out that they could buy these clothes and sell them at the Barras and make a killing. They worked out how much money they had between them and went into the shop in a businesslike manner and said to the shop assistant., 'We'll take 50 suits, 100 shirts and 50 pairs of trousers.'

The shop assistant started to laugh and asked them if they were from Glasgow.

The two Weegies were not happy about this and were thinking of giving the assistant a Glesga kiss but they really wanted the suits, shirts and trousers so they just asked, 'How did ye know that?'

The shop assistant replied, 'This is a dry cleaners!'

The Demon Drink

Robbie was a staunch teetotaller and so was his father. There was no drink allowed in their house. Then Robbie met a bonny lassie called Annie and they fell in love and got engaged. The next thing was to break this news to his parents as Annie owned a popular pub on the outskirts of Edinburgh and that's where they would live when they got married.

His father and mother liked Annie but were not very happy when their son told them that when they were married he would have to take a friendly drink with his customers.

His father said that this was certainly a dilemma for such a staunch teetotal family and he would have to sleep on it.

The next day his father announced, 'Weel, Robbie, your mother and I can see what a sore temptation being with all that drink will be to ye but we ken fine that business is business sae we see nae harm in ye havin' a wee drink wi' yir customers – so lang as ye dinnae enjoy it!'

....

Andy's mother wis fair scunnered with his new teacher at his school in Edinburgh. She'd never had sae much bother wi' his homework before so she decided enough was enough and she sent wee Andy to school with a note which said:

'It's no Andy's fault that he hisnae done the sum you gave him aboot how lang it wid take tae walk from Edinburgh tae Aberdeen as it is too far. The last time you asked how lang it wid take tae walk five times from the Castle to Holyrood, his father lost a morning's work and after all his walking you marked the sum wrong.'

....

Mrs Campbell thought she should take more interest in her husband's activities so she decided to start by going fishing with him.

Her friends asked her how she got on and she said, 'Weel then, I made every mistake in the book! First of all I talked too much, then I used the wrong bait, then I talked too loud and then I reeled in too soon. To make matters even worse, I caught more fish than he did!'

....

'Dae you no think it's time we got married, Tommy? We been going out together now for nearly twenty years'

'Aye, lass. Ah'm thinking the same myself. Ah'm thinking we ought tae get married.'

Jeannie's eyes lit up and her heart started thumping in anticipation when Tommy continued, 'But Ah dinnae ken anyone that would have us.'

RECIPES

TASTY SCOTTISH TREATS FOR ALL TO EAT!

Shortbread Petticoat Tails

SHUTTERSTOCK/CURLY COURLAND

See **page 24** for recipe

Cock-a-leekie Soup

COCK-A-LEEKIE SOUP This is a warming winter soup and it is often served as a starter at a Burns Supper. It is traditionally made by boiling a cockerel and leeks and adding prunes but if the prunes are not to your liking leave them out. It can also be made with an oven-ready chicken as in this recipe.

INGREDIENTS:

1.4 kg (3 lb) oven-ready chicken
2 onions, roughly chopped
1.7 litres (3 pints) water
25g (1 oz) butter
900g (2 lb) leeks, cleaned and cut into 1-inch pieces
450g (1 lb) carrots, cleaned, peeled and chopped
125g (4 oz) ready-to-eat pitted prunes, sliced
Salt and pepper to taste
Bouquet garni of bay leaf, parsley, thyme

PREPARATION:

1. Put the chicken in a large saucepan and add the onions and bouquet garni.
2. Add the water and bring to the boil and then reduce the heat, cover and simmer gently for one hour and 20 minutes or until the chicken is well cooked.
3. Remove the chicken from the saucepan, strain the stock and set aside.
4. Strip the chicken from the bones and chop up.
5. Add the chicken, the leeks, the carrots and the prunes to the strained stock, adding more water as necessary.
6. Bring the soup to the boil and season to taste. Cover with a lid and simmer for about 30 minutes.

KEDGEREE It may seem a bit strange to use curry powder in a traditional Scottish recipe but Scottish regiments served in India and presumably they enjoyed the flavour and brought the recipe back home. This dish of smoked fish, rice and curry powder proved to be popular and is still served today, sometimes topped with a poached egg instead of adding hard-boiled eggs to the ingredients.

INGREDIENTS: To serve four people

2 fillets of smoked haddock or herring, bones and skin removed
2 hard-boiled eggs
350g (¾ lb) long grain basmati rice or brown rice
300ml (10 floz) milk
50g (2oz) butter
750ml (1¼ pints) chicken stock
1 Small onion
1 or **2** bay leaves
Chopped parsley
One teaspoon curry powder
Half teaspoon grated nutmeg
Ground pepper

PREPARATION:

1. Pre-heat the oven to 180°C, gas mark 4.
2. Place the chopped onion and butter in an oven-proof dish and cook gently on the hob, adding the rice and stirring to coat it with butter.
3. Add the bay leaf and stock and bring to the boil.
4. Cover and cook in the oven for about 20 minutes or until the rice has absorbed the stock.
5. Remove the bay leaf at the end of cooking.
6. Heat the milk in a pan on the hob (don't boil), add the fish and poach for five minutes until cooked and then drain off the liquid and flake the fish.
7. When the rice is ready, use a fork to stir in the flaked fish, chopped eggs, curry powder, nutmeg and pepper.

Kedgeree

SHUTTERSTOCK/CURLY COURLAND

PETTICOAT TAILS are made of shortbread, which is not a bread but a sweet biscuit. The liberal amount of butter in the recipe makes the shortbread rich and causes it to shatter into flaky layers. This process is called shortening. It is said that Mary, Queen of Scots was very partial to *les petites gatelles* (little cakes) and the name petticoat tails is, perhaps, a corruption of this.

INGREDIENTS:
110g (4 oz) butter (if you use unsalted butter, add a pinch of salt to the mixture)
50g (2 oz) caster sugar
110g (4 oz) plain flour
50g (2 oz) cornflour

PREPARATION:
1. Pre-heat oven to 160°C, gas mark 3.
2. Cream the butter until it is soft and then add the caster sugar.
3. Beat the mixture until it becomes pale and creamy.
4. Sieve the plain flour and the cornflour together and lightly combine; add the salt, if required.
5. Add the flour mixture, about one-third at a time, to the butter and sugar mixture, and combine. The mixture should be quite stiff.
6. Put the mixture on a large baking tray and roll out the mixture to form a 20 cm (8 inch) circle.
7. Use a spoon handle to press indentations around the edge of the mixture and then use a fork to prick the mixture.
8. Using a knife, score each round into 10 or 12 even wedges.
9. Sprinkle with a little caster sugar. Leave to chill in the fridge for 15 minutes and then bake in the oven for 30 minutes or until a pale, golden colour.
10. Cool on a wire rack for about 5 minutes and, while still warm, cut gently through the score marks. Leave to cool and store in an airtight tin.

MURDERS

The Maggie Dickson's Pub in Grassmarket

HALF-HANGIT MAGGIE

Maggie Dickson lived in Musselburgh and worked as a salt seller. Her husband was press-ganged into the navy in 1723 and she became pregnant with another man's child. This was a humiliating experience in those days so Maggie hid all signs of her condition. The baby died and Maggie was tried and found guilty of a capital crime under the 1690 Concealment of Pregnancy Act and sentenced to be hanged. The hanging took place on 2nd September 1724 in the Grassmarket and many people came to watch, as every hanging attracted a crowd. The hangman, John Dalgliesh, forgot to tie her hands and as she grabbed at the noose Dalgliesh beat her with a stick and tugged at her legs to hasten her death. She was placed in her coffin and, as usual, surgeon-apprentices were lying in wait to snatch the corpse for dissection. A scuffle broke out between them and Maggie's family, during which the coffin lid was damaged. As a result it did not fit properly and this allowed air to enter her coffin. During the journey home, the family stopped at Peffer Mill and noises were heard coming from the coffin, where Maggie was found to be alive. The Edinburgh officials had to consider this case. Should Maggie be returned to the scaffold to be hanged once again? After some deliberation it was decided that no one could be hanged twice so she was free to go. She became known as 'Half-hangit Maggie' and a pub in the Grassmarket still bears her name.

GEORGE BRYCE (D. 1864)

When George Bryce was working at Ratho Villa he met Isabella Brown, a young servant girl. The other servants disapproved of this relationship and the nursemaid Jane Seton advised young Isabella not to get tangled up with George. Isabella then broke off her relationship and this angered George. He broke into Jane's room and, although she tried to escape, Bryce caught her and slit her throat with a razor and poor Jane bled to death. As there were witnesses to this callous deed Bryce could not deny the charge of murder so he pleaded insanity. However, he was sentenced to death by hanging.

The execution took place in Edinburgh on 21st June 1864. In 1784, the trap door mechanism had been introduced and this caused the condemned person's neck to break at the end of the fall, resulting in a crushed windpipe, so death should have been quick. The hangman was Thomas Askem from York and it appears that he fixed a drop that was too short, and Bryce swung on the rope and was slowly strangled. It was forty minutes before he was declared dead and the crowd of over 25,000 were outraged and turned on Askem, who had to be protected by the police, given a disguise and smuggled out of the city. This was the last public execution in the city of Edinburgh. Executions were then carried out in a purpose-built cell in Calton Prison.

JOHN PORTEOUS (C.1695–1736)

Born in the Burgh of Canongate, Porteous rose to the rank of captain in the city guard by 1726. In April 1736, Porteous was on duty when a condemned smuggler, Andrew Wilson, was hanged in the Grassmarket. It was thought that there was a plan to rescue the body as there were many ways to cheat the hangman's noose so long as the body was cut down quickly. The crowd threw stones at the city guard as a distraction while Wilson's body was cut down and attempts were made to resuscitate him. This incident turned into a riot outside the Tolbooth which was, in those days, near St Giles' Cathedral in the High Street.

The Mercat Cross on the Royal Mile SHUTTERSTOCK/PLUSONE

who lived in the adjacent tenements. The riot escalated and shots were fired into the mob, killing six people.

Porteous was tried for murder, found guilty and sentenced to be executed in the Grassmarket on 8th September 1736. He appealed to Sir Robert Walpole, the first British Prime Minister, and the death sentence was deferred. Furious that he might get acquitted, over 4,000 protesters attacked the Tolbooth and dragged Porteous from his cell to the Grassmarket where he was stripped naked, beaten and his arms and legs broken. Then he was burned before being hanged on a dyer's pole. Sir Walter Scott's novel, *The Heart of Midlothian*, published in 1818, starts with the Porteous riots.

JESSIE KING AND THE MURDERERS UNDER THE CAR PARK

Jessie King made a living by taking

The 'Heart of Midlothian' set in the cobbles near St Giles' Cathedral marks the entrance to the Old Tolbooth Prison SHUTTERSTOCK/STOCKCUBE

Porteous retaliated when the mob stoned the Tolbooth and ordered his men to fire over the heads of the crowd. However, the shots were aimed too high and wounded people in laundry and children. She lived in Canonmills and then in Cheyne Street in Stockbridge and watched the newspapers for adverts from desperate women with illegitimate children who were looking for people to adopt them. Jessie would offer to take the children as long as she was also given a sum of money for their upkeep. Jessie kept the money but disposed of the children. Baby farmers like Jessie would charge between £2 and £5 to look after a baby 'for life'.

Jessie was caught when some boys found a partially burnt oilskin package and kicked it around. To their horror it burst open and there was the body of one-year-old Alexander Gunn. When the police raided the Kings' house they found the strangled body of Violet Thompson, who was only a few months old. Jessie was tried and sentenced to death and she was hanged at Calton Gaol on 11th March 1880. There were crowds outside

81 George Street where the Chantrelle family lived

the gaol as hangings no longer took place in public. Jules Verne visited the gaol in 1859 and said it resembled a small-scale version of a medieval town. Calton Gaol was demolished in the 1930s and the prisoners moved to Saughton prison. The door to the Calton death cell can be found in the Beehive Inn in the Grassmarket.

Some of the bodies of those hanged at Calton were buried in the grounds of the gaol. When St Andrew's House was built on this site, the car park was built over their graves. Jessie King's body still lies under this car park along with others including Eugene Marie Chantrelle, hanged in 1878 for murdering his wife; Robert Vickers and William Innes, two Gorebridge miners hanged in 1884 for killing a gamekeeper; John Herdman, hanged in 1898 for murdering his girlfriend Jane Calder; Patrick Higgins, hanged in 1913 for murdering his two sons, William and John; John Henry Savage,

St Andrew's House

hanged in 1923 for the murder of Jemma Grierson; Philip Murray, hanged in 1923 for killing William Cree by throwing him out of a window when he found him with his wife.

WILLIAM BURKE (1792–1829) AND WILLIAM HARE (BORN BETWEEN 1792 AND 1804)

Both Burke and Hare were Irish and they both ended up working in Scotland and eventually moving to Edinburgh, where their paths crossed. In 1827, Burke and his wife Nelly had lodgings at the 'Beggars' Hotel' in Portsburgh but when the hotel burnt down they moved to Brown's Close in the Grassmarket.

In the meantime Hare had taken lodgings in Tanner's Close in Edinburgh and there is a possibility that he disposed of his landlord before moving in with the man's wife, Maggie. The pair now ran the lodging house, where they crammed up to twenty-four lodgers in eight beds, charging thruppence a night. Burke and Nelly ended up moving into Tanner's Close with the Hares. In November 1827, one of

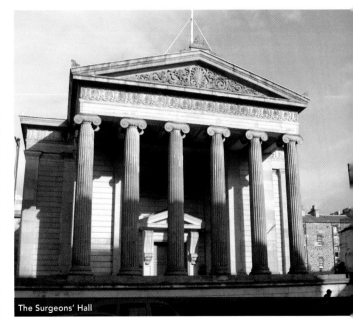

The Surgeons' Hall

the lodgers, an elderly man called Donald, died before he paid his rent so Hare asked Burke to help him place the body in a sack and sell it to Professor Robert Knox (1791–1862) for dissection. They were pleased to make a profit from the deal as Knox paid them nearly twice as much as the rent arrears. Rather than wait on opportune deaths, they invited people to the lodging house, got them drunk and suffocated them using a sticky plaster of tar which left no marks on the body, making it suitable for Knox to dissect. Burke and Hare went on to murder about thirty more victims within the next few months.

When Margery Campbell was murdered in October 1828, suspicions were aroused, and when the police found her body in Knox's cellar, Burke and Hare were charged with murder. Hare turned King's evidence and was set free. He got a job at a lime factory but when his identity was discovered the workers threw lime in his face and he ended his life as a blind beggar, possibly in London. No record can be found of his death.

Burke was hanged at the top of Liberton's Wynd in the Lawnmarket on 28th January 1829, watched by a crowd of over 20,000, including Sir Walter Scott. Burke's body was taken for dissection and his skeleton is now in the Edinburgh University Anatomy Museum.

Edinburgh doctors were allowed to dissect dead criminals but they could never get enough of them for their experiments. Burke and Hare were not body-snatchers but murderers. The body-snatchers dug up graves to steal bodies and because of this families started to have their relatives buried under iron cages. Robert Louis Stevenson wrote *The Body Snatcher*, based on the students who worked for Knox.

CLANS AND TARTANS

TARTAN IS A DESCRIPTION OF HOW THE **THREAD** IS WOVEN TO MAKE THE **CLOTH**.

The Sporran SHUTTERSTOCK/JANE RIX

Each thread is passed over two threads then under two threads. The difference between a check and tartan is that the check square shows only one colour and in tartan there are always squares when the thread colours cross. When the thread was woven into cloth it was waulked by wetting, pulling, beating and stretching the tartan into shape across a wooden frame. Like many others doing jobs that demanded a rhythm to their physical labour, the workers would sing, usually in Gaelic, and here are a few translated verses of a waulking song.

Carmina Gadelica by **Alexander Carmichael** *(1832–1912).*

The wool is carded, washed and dyed,

The ember heat and reeking peat

Pervade and cense the house inside,

Wall shadows in the gloom.

The threads of yellow, blue and green,

The black, the red, the white,

By fingers deft in warp and weft,

A criss-cross sett is laid between

To form the cloth aright.

The fulling at the waulking frame,

The maidens all a-row,

On either side sit well supplied,

With love-songs ready to exclaim,

In movements to and fro.

King George II's Dress Act banned the wearing of Highland dress and the penalties for disobeying included deportation for seven years. Only the army could wear the kilt and the Black Watch regimental tartan.

Statue of King George IV SHUTTERSTOCK/ PSD PHOTOGRAPH

In 1822, King George IV visited Edinburgh on the invitation of the Chair of the Celtic Society of Edinburgh, Sir Walter Scott, who declared that for this special occasion 'let every man wear his tartan'. The visit encouraged clans (families) to be identified with a particular sett (pattern) and by the end of the 1800s all the recognised clans in Scotland had their own tartans.

Queen Victoria was a supporter of Highland dress and her home at Balmoral had many tartan furnishings. There is etiquette to wearing tartan; no one outside of the Royal Family should wear the Balmoral and Chief's tartans should be worn only by the Chief and his immediate family. The old Hunting Stewart tartan is now regarded as a universal tartan, as are the modern Flower of Scotland and Pride of Scotland tartans. To find out if you have a family tartan visit **www.tartans.scotland.net.**

Balmoral Castle SHUTTERSTOCK/PATRICIA HOFMEESTER

WALKS

TIME TO STRETCH THOSE LEGS!

St Giles' Cathedral

OLD TOWN WALK

Start outside **St Giles' Cathedral** on the **Royal Mile** and look at the cobblestones where you will see the Heart of Midlothian and some brass markings that show where the Old Tolbooth stood. It was **Sir Walter Scott** who first called this spot The Heart of Midlothian in his novel.

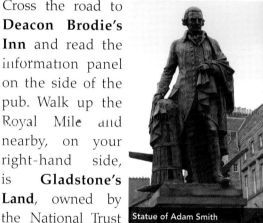
Statue of Adam Smith

Cross the road to **Deacon Brodie's Inn** and read the information panel on the side of the pub. Walk up the Royal Mile and nearby, on your right-hand side, is **Gladstone's Land**, owned by the National Trust for Scotland. It is a good example of a land or high-rise building with a luckenbooth downstairs and living accommodation above. Cross over and take a look in **Riddell's Court** where **David Hume**, the philosopher,

Riddle's Court

once lived. Now walk back down this side of the Royal Mile, taking a look at **Brodie's Court** where **Deacon Brodie** lived and then turn right along **George IV Bridge**. A little way along here on your right is the **Elephant House**, a café favoured by writers such as **Ian Rankin**, **Alexander McCall Smith** and **J.K. Rowling** who wrote some of *Harry Potter* here. Further along on the same side is the statue of **Greyfriars Bobby**, with a shiny nose as passers-by rub it for luck. Behind is Greyfriars Bobby's Bar and to the side of the pub is Greyfriars Kirkyard, where ghostly things are said to occur.

Cross the road and walk along **Chambers Street**. In the middle of the street is a statue of **William Chambers**, who was Lord Provost of Edinburgh from 1856 to 1869. Cross over to the **Museum of Scotland**, a child-friendly museum with a brasserie, gift shop and toilets. Continue along to the T-junction with **South Bridge**. Just on the right is **Old College**, the site of the original buildings of Edinburgh University. This walk now turns left along **South Bridge**; however, along on the right is the **Black Medicine Coffee Company**, another haunt of J.K.

John Knox House

Rowling, and the **Surgeon's Hall Museum** with its **Burke and Hare** connection.

Along **South Bridge** on your left, just past Sainsbury's, look down into

Canongate Tolbooth

Cowgate and the entrance to Blair Street where you can book a tour of the ghostly South Bridge Vaults at **Mercat Tours**. This view shows what a multi-layered city this is. At the junction with

Royal Mile is the **Tron Church**. Turn right here and walk down the **Royal Mile**. You will pass **Niddry Street**, where the **Banshee Labyrinth** boasts of being the most haunted pub in Scotland, and further along is the **Museum of Childhood**. Do take time to peek into the old closes, some being more attractive than others. **John Knox House** is on the left-hand side and the **World's End pub** at the corner

'High-rise' Tenement on the Royal Mile

of **St Mary's Street** was where the old city boundary ended. Number 2 St Mary's Street was the first building erected under the 1867 Improvement Act. You are now in **Canongate**. On your right is **Chessell's Court**, where **Deacon Brodie** tried his hand at robbing the Excise House. **Old Playhouse Close** was once a popular theatre venue and opposite **St John's Close** is the **Fudge House** where the Di Sotto family have been making fudge by hand since 1949. The **Canongate Tolbooth** and the **People's Museum** is next door to **Canongate Kirk and Kirkyard**. Striding along the pavement is poet **Robert Fergusson** of 'Auld Reikie' fame. Turn left into **Dunbar's Close** and explore these lovely hidden gardens. A little further along is **Panmure Close** where **Adam Smith** lived but you need to continue along and go through the arches beside the newsagents to see his old house. Further along is the **Kilderkin Pub** where **Golfer's Land**, built with James Patterson's winnings from playing golf, once stood. **White Horse Close** on the left used to be where stagecoaches departed for Newcastle and London. At the roundabout you have a choice of visiting the **Scottish Parliament** designed by **Enric Miralles** *(1955–2000)*, **Holyrood Palace**, the Queen's Gallery or **Dynamic Earth**. Our walk ends here, but on another day you can walk up Edinburgh's volcano to **Arthur's Seat** and explore the 640-acre **Holyrood Park**.

The Scottish Parliament

NEW TOWN WALK

The Scott Monument

Start in Princes Street Gardens at the **Scott Monument**, a memorial to **Sir Walter Scott**, with amazing views from the top if you are willing to climb the 287 steps. Walk through the gardens, which used to be the stinking Nor' Loch, until you came to the **National Galleries** on your left. Cross here at the traffic lights and walk up **Hanover Street** to the statue of **King George IV** who was welcomed to Edinburgh by Sir Walter Scott. Turn left along **George Street** and look out for the **Old Assembly Rooms**, now a restaurant. Numbers 51 and 81 were both lived in by the Chantrelle family. Eugene Chantrelle was hanged at Calton Jail in 1878 for murdering his wife, Elizabeth,

by poisoning her with opium. Take a look at the lighthouse above number 84. Cross **Castle Street** and walk along to number 30 where **Kenneth Grahame**, author of *The Wind in the Willows*, was born in 1859. Go back to **George Street**, and cross over to

Statue of Prince Albert in Charlotte Square

North Castle Street. **Sir Walter Scott** lived at number 39 for over twenty years. Return to **George Street** and continue towards **Charlotte Square** with its private garden dominated by a statue of Prince Albert and, behind,

Sphynx and lums in Charlotte Square

West Register House, part of the National Archives of Scotland, in what was previously St George's Church. Number 7 is the National Trust for Scotland's **Georgian House**.

Keep left at Charlotte Square and enter **South Charlotte Street**; number 14 is where **Alexander Graham Bell** was born. Return to **Charlotte Square**, cross **George Street** and take the first on your right into **Young Street** with its Cambridge Bar and further along the **Oxford Bar**, the haunt of crime writer Ian Rankin and his famous character, Inspector Rebus. Turn left into **North Castle Street** and right into **Queen Street. Sir James Young Simpson** *(1811–70)*, who discovered the anaesthetic properties of chloroform, lived at number 52. At the traffic lights cross over into **Queen Street Gardens West**. Queen Street Gardens are privately owned by residents and are divided into sections, each with their own rules. Turn right into **Heriot Row**. On the garden railings you will see some information about **Robert Louis Stevenson**, author of many books including

The Oxford Bar in Young Street

Treasure Island, who lived opposite in number 17. Go back and turn right into **Howe Street**, where there are some classy shops, and then turn right into **Northumberland Street**. This is a lovely street with wide, colourful doors, period lighting and balconies. Enjoy walking along here and peek down the lanes and you will see some buildings that in times past were used for stabling horses and carriages. Turn left into **Dundas Street** with its galleries and antique shops and right along **Great King Street. Thomas**

Once the home of Sir James Young Simpson

de Quincey author of *Confessions of an English Opium-Eater*, once lived at number 9 and **J.M. Barrie**, author of *Peter Pan*, lived at number 3. **Drummond Place** also has a private garden. Walk around, keeping the garden on your right-hand side, and you will pass **Scotland Street**, the setting for **Alexander McCall Smith's** *44 Scotland Street* stories of child prodigy Bertie and Cyril the dog. On the corner, 31 Drummond

Queen Street Gardens

Drummond Place

of artist **Sir Henry Raeburn**. Cross **Broughton Street** into **Picardy Place** and there is a plaque on number 2 stating that **Sir Arthur Conan Doyle** was born at number 11 and a statue of **Sherlock Holmes**. Cross over to the **Conan Doyle Pub** where this walk ends. From here you can choose shopping in John Lewis and the St James Centre, a walk up Calton Hill or to go along Leith Walk and turn up Waterloo Place to the Old Calton Burial Ground, which is famous for its many memorials and graves, including the Political Martyrs' Monument.

Place was once the home of **Compton Mackenzie**, author of *Whisky Galore*. Continue round, crossing London Street and turning left down **Dublin Street**. When you come to **Abercromby Place** on your right take a glance down here as it was the first curved street built in the New Town and **Marie Stopes** *(1880–1958)* lived at number 3. Continue along Dublin Street to the T-junction and facing you is the **Portrait Gallery**. Turn left here and **32 York Place** was once the home

32 York Place

TALES OF THE SUPERNATURAL TO **CHILL THE BLOOD...**

SHUTTERSTOCK/ANNA KUCHEROVA

'Here are the ghosts of Edinburgh, here in these old stone courtyards, in these dim wynds and closes where pale, insignificant lamps hang above flights of grey stairs, the mighty history of this city stirs a little in its sleep. It is grey, sinister, and mediaeval'.

H.V. Morgan, 1920

THE LOST PIPER AND THE GHOSTLY DRUMMER

A series of secret tunnels run from Edinburgh Castle down the Royal Mile and perhaps even to the Palace of Holyroodhouse where Mary, Queen of Scots, lived between 1561 and 1567. When these tunnels were rediscovered about a hundred years ago, a piper was sent down to walk through the tunnels, playing his bagpipes. By following the strains of the music above ground a map could be made of the tunnels. However, about halfway down the Royal Mile the skirling of the pipes came to a sudden stop. Despite search parties scouring the tunnels, the piper was never seen again. However, it is said that the ghost of this piper still walks endlessly through the tunnels and sometimes, on a misty day, strains of the pipes can be heard coming from beneath the Royal Mile.

In 1650, a soldier on sentry duty at Edinburgh Castle heard the sound of a drummer approaching. He challenged the drummer, although he could not see him as the night was dark and foggy. When no answer was heard, the soldier fired his musket at the ghostly shape emerging through the gloom. Soldiers searched for the drummer but he was never found.

This happened more than once and eventually the drumming was accompanied by the clanking of armour and the sound of soldiers marching. The army took these events as a forewarning of an invasion. In the September of 1650, Oliver Cromwell laid siege to the castle and, after three months of conflict, Edinburgh Castle surrendered to Cromwell's army.

JOHNNY ONE-ARM

John Chiesly's divorce case was heard by Sir George Lockhart, Lord President of the Court of Session, and he ordered Chiesly to pay his wife and eleven children £93 a year. In a rage about the verdict Chiesly swore revenge on Sir George. True to his word, Chiesly shot Lockhart dead when he was on his way home from the kirk on Easter Sunday, 1689. Chiesly was caught and in order to find out if he acted alone or with accomplices, he was tortured with thumbscrews and booties at the Mercat Cross in Edinburgh, but he

Advocate's Court

would not confess to anyone else being involved. Chiesly was then tried and sentenced to be hanged. While he was still alive, the hand he used to fire the pistol was cut off and stuck on a spike at the West Port. The rest of his body was suspended in chains with the pistol hung around his neck. After a while his body mysteriously disappeared and the ghost of Johnny One-Arm haunted Dalry, terrifying people with its screaming and hysterical laughter. In 1965 workmen found the skeleton of a man with many broken bones, a pistol round his neck and no right hand, behind the hearth in a cottage in Dalry Park. After Chiesly's body was given a proper burial, the ghost of Johnny One-Arm was never seen again.

THE REAL MARY KING'S CLOSE

Mary King's Close is a rare survivor of medieval Edinburgh. In 1645, the plague struck this narrow close and the council tried to stop the disease from spreading by bricking up the

The Real Mary King's Close

close with the plague victims still alive inside. These streets are preserved as the Royal Exchange was built on top of Mary King's Close. This is an undeniably creepy place and visitors often leave gifts for a wee girl called Annie whose spirit still haunts these subterranean streets as she searches for her favourite doll. Feelings of unease are often experienced by the hundreds of visitors, and orbs, odd mists and other light anomalies have been picked up by cameras. Paranormal activity was first reported here centuries ago. Mr Thomas Coltheart was one of the few people to risk moving back into Mary King's Close after the plague had subsided and he found the area to be scarily haunted. He claimed he and his family became the victims of considerable disturbance, unsettling poltergeist activity and the startling appearance of disembodied hands and heads. In a weird twist of fate, Coltheart himself became a ghost and his form was seen by a number of witnesses after his death. The Real Mary King's Close is now a tourist attraction so you can walk along this warren of 17th-century streets that are buried deep beneath the Royal Mile and see for yourself what it was really like for the people who lived, worked and died here, and perhaps experience a shiver down your spine!

THE SOUTH BRIDGE VAULTS

The South Bridge Vaults are chambers formed by the nineteen arches of the bridge, built in 1788. Disused and forgotten, they were rediscovered only in the 1980s. Tradesmen originally occupied them but as the chambers deteriorated the businesses moved out and taverns and brothels moved in. It is said that Burke and Hare may have hunted for victims amongst these dark, dank tunnels and also stored the murdered bodies somewhere within these 120 vaults that lie beneath the surface of South Bridge.

The South Bridge Vaults ©MERCAT TOURS

The Vaults on the North Side of the Cowgate arch form a series of tunnels and these are especially spooky, so they are often used for ghost tours. Ghost spotting is not new here as after the 1824 fire in the Vaults, there was talk of a South Bridge poltergeist.

Since the Vaults re-opened in 1996 there has been a catalogue of ghostly experiences, presences and apparitions including the ghost of the Watcher, a 17th-century gentleman in a long cloak. Visitors sometimes find themselves pushed by an invisible force in one of the chambers and a gang of builders fled in panic after they were pelted with stones. Dr Richard Wiseman of the University of Hertfordshire ran an investigation, monitoring the experiences of volunteers who spent hours alone in these chambers. One volunteer reported hearing breathing and another saw a figure wearing an apron. Variations in magnetic fields and air movements were recorded from these haunted chambers. You can book a tour of the South Bridge Vaults through Mercat Tours in Blair Street.

THE GHOST OF DEACON WILLIAM BRODIE (1741–88)

Chessell's Court where the Excise House once stood

Brodie's Close, off Lawnmarket, was named after William Brodie's father and it is where the family lived in a very fine town house. The respectable family business of cabinet-making was lucrative and Brodie inherited a substantial amount of money and property on his father's death. As a

Deacon and Town Councillor, Brodie was an influential businessman. However, he led a double life and frequented Edinburgh's dens of iniquity. A compulsive gambler and enthralled by cock-fighting, he was deceitful and manipulating. He kept a wife and two mistresses who, conveniently, all lived nearby, with his wife in Brodie's Close, a mistress and three children in Cant's Close and, in Libberton's Wynd, a second mistress and two sons.

Brodie turned to burglary, making impressions of customers' and business acquaintances' keys by using putty, and Michael Henderson, a locksmith in Grassmarket, filed the keys. Brodie and his accomplices burgled many Edinburgh houses and, desiring greater adventure, he entered Edinburgh University and stole their silver mace, then burgled the Excise Office and the Royal Exchange. Eventually Brodie was caught, tried and sentenced to hanging. An inveterate gambler, he tried to cheat death by having a silver tube inserted in his throat to prevent his windpipe being crushed. His body was whipped away by friends after the hanging so perhaps he did survive!

His spirit certainly lives on as he was the inspiration for Robert Louis Stevenson's popular novel, *The Strange Case of Dr Jekyll and Mr Hyde (1886)* and his ghost, a shadowy figure carrying a lantern, appears to haunt the narrow wynds off Castle Hill.

SPOOKY GREYFRIARS

Poor little Bobby, the little Skye terrier, mourned his master, John Gray, by spending fourteen years by Auld Jock's grave in Greyfriars Kirkyard. When Bobby died in 1872, he was not allowed to be buried beside John Gray because he was a dog, so for the first time in his life he was separated from his master. A statue of Greyfriars Bobby is mounted

Greyfriars Bobby Pub

Nowadays Greyfriars is as well known for its spooks as it is for the sad tale of Greyfriars Bobby. There are regular ghost tours held in the churchyard and many people have reported unpleasant experiences in the southern part of the cemetery around the area of the Covenanters' Prison. It was here in the 17th century that many people who sought religious independence were locked up on suspicion of treason and these men, women and children were treated so harshly that many of them died. Many visitors to the graveyard claim to have experienced overwhelming feelings of dread and nausea and have even passed out. Others claim to have been pushed, slapped or pinched by something invisible, particularly near the monument to Sir George Mackenzie of Rosehaugh (1636–91), the man responsible for the covenanters' fate. 'Bloody' Mackenzie's mausoleum has long been considered to be haunted and a weird, glowing, spooky figure has also been reported here.

on a granite fountain and can be found on George IV Bridge, just outside the kirkyard.

The Kirk of the Greyfriars was the first church built in Edinburgh after the reformation and permission for the kirkyard was granted in 1562.

LOCAL CUSTOMS

SHUTTERSTOCK/KANUMAN

Hogmanay

Torchlight Procession SHUTTERSTOCK/BRENDAN HOWARD

New Year's Eve in Edinburgh is a time for celebration. Edinburgh's Hogmanay celebrations take place over three days and start with a spectacular torchlight procession and fireworks on 30th December. On Hogmanay, the city seems to be just one big street party, with concerts in Princes Street Gardens and a great atmosphere. Tens of thousands of tickets are sold to residents and visitors from around the globe every year. As the bells strike midnight, fireworks explode, lighting up the skies above Edinburgh, and the Auld Reekie partygoers sing *Auld Lang Syne*. Here are a couple

AULD LANG SYNE
by RABBIE BURNS *(1759–96)*

Should auld acquaintance be forgot,

And never brought to mind?

Should auld acquaintance be forgot,

And auld lang syne

Chorus:

For auld land syne, my dear,

For auld lang syne

We'll tak a cup o' kindness yet,

For auld lang syne!

And here's my hand my trusty fiere,

And gies a hand o' thine,

We'll tak a right guid-willie waught,

For auld lang syne.

of verses. When you sing 'And here's my hand…' cross your arms and join hands with anybody on either side of you. If it was less crowded and you were in the normal circle, you would run or stagger into the middle and out again – still holding hands!

This song has gained an international reputation and has been sung in many places around the world. An American teacher, Luther Whiting Mason, introduced *Auld Lang Syne* to the school curriculum in Japan in the 1890s and nowadays it is played there in some shops and restaurants at closing time. **Shirley Temple** sang this song to a dying soldier in the 1937 film, *Wee Willie Winkie* and there was not a dry eye in the house. It also features in Frank Capra's 1946 film, *It's a Wonderful Life* and in the 2008 movie, *Sex and the City*.

BURNS SUPPER

This is a celebration of the Scottish poet, Rabbie Burns. There is a formality to this event which has been held on 25th January for over 200 years, with some suppers being more formal than others. If there is a high table then the other guests are obliged to stand while the piper plays and the high table is seated. Everyone is welcomed and the *Selkirk Grace* is said before the supper:

Haggis, neeps and tatties

SHUTTERSTOCK/NORMAN POGSON

Some hae meat and canna eat,

Some hae nane that wunt it,

But we hae meat and we can eat,

And sae the Lord be thankit

The haggis, carried on a silver platter, is piped in and it is usual to stand for this. The haggis is then addressed by the recitation of Burn's poem *To a Haggis*. The reader of the poem should have his skean dhu at the ready as when he comes to 'An out you up wi' ready sleight' he cuts open the haggis, 'Trenching your gushing entrails bright'. At the end of the poem there is a toast to the haggis. Supper is then served and, traditionally, it consists of cock-a-leekie soup, haggis with bashed neeps an' champit tatties, followed by Typsy Laird, which is a sherry trifle.

Entertainment follows and a few Burns songs are sung such as *My Luve is Like a Red, Red, Rose* and *Ae Fond Kiss*. A few poems follow, the most popular being *Tam O' Shanter*. This is followed by a speech to The Immortal Memory of Burns, a Toast to the Lassies followed by a Reply to the Toast to the Lassies, and the evening ends with everyone singing *Auld Lang Syne*.

The Burns Monument, Calton Hill, Edinburgh was erected in 1830 by Thomas Hamilton to commemorate Scotland's national poet Robert Burns SHUTTERSTOCK/NORMAN POGSON

The Edinburgh Tattoo

SHUTTERSTOCK/MORAG FLEMING

THE EDINBURGH FESTIVAL

The first Edinburgh International Festival took place in 1947. It was directed by Rudolf Bing of the Glyndebourne Opera, working alongside the British Council in Scotland and civic leaders from the City of Edinburgh. This was a pioneering event and the first festival of its kind in the world. Now, over sixty years later, this Festival, which takes place in August and September, is firmly established.

The first Festival was 'gate-crashed' by eight theatre groups who were not invited to take part and so were not on the programme of events. These keen actors were not put off by this and staged their own shows anywhere they could find a venue; this was the start of the Edinburgh Festival Fringe. The first International Film Festival was also held in Edinburgh in 1947 and today, in June, it attracts big names and cutting-edge talent to its programme of screenings, talks and events. The Royal Edinburgh Military Tattoo is held at Edinburgh Castle in August and is watched by 100 million people on television every year.

The Edinburgh Fringe – stilt walker on the Royal Mile SHUTTERSTOCK/JAN KRANENDONK

LOCAL SPORTS

A way of celebrating Scottish and Celtic culture and heritage

HIGHLAND GAMES

It is possible that, originally, these games were a showcase of talents including strength, bravery and swiftness as well as Highland dancing and playing the bagpipes. The Clan Chieftain could then choose the fittest fighters, the strongest bodyguards, and the best entertainers to while away the dark winter evenings. Clans would compete against each other in all of these events and many of these traditional sports can be watched today. There are small Highland Games held not very far from Edinburgh and larger events such as

SHUTTERSTOCK/RUTH BLACK

SHUTTERSTOCK/DAVID HUGHES

the Braemar Gathering, which attracts about 10,000 spectators and is always held on the first Saturday in September. Some of the sports you might see are:

TOSSING THE CABER

The caber is a long, heavy, trimmed tree trunk about 6 metres in length although the lengths do vary quite a bit. It is placed on end, the thickest end at the top. The competitor crouches down and wedges the caber between his neck and shoulder and picks it up with his hands holding the base. He tosses it so that it turns with the thick end touching the ground first. The caber should fall away from the tosser. It is not the distance that matters but the angle that the caber falls relative to the thrower.

THROWING THE HAMMER

Became an event at the Highland Games in the 18th century and although similar to the modern hammer throw there are some differences. Here a round metal ball is attached to the end of a shaft about 4 feet (1.2 metres) in length. The hammer is swung around the head and thrown over the shoulder for the furthest possible distance.

PUTTING THE STONE

This is similar to the shot-put but here a large stone is often used instead of a steel shot, and there are different rules on the techniques allowed to throw the stone.

Stamp celebrating the **Braemar Gathering**

SHUTTERSTOCK/NEFTALI

THE HARRIERS

There are many local Harrier groups such as the Edinburgh Hash House Harriers where running is non-competitive and fun. Hashing is a combination of running, orienteering and partying. The 'hare' has a head start and marks the way using chalk, flour or paper trails through the occasional street but mostly through woods, fields and footpaths. The harriers give chase and at the end of the trail there is always a party.

SHINTY

Shinty is a high-speed, full contact team game and Scotland's national sport. It is often described as a cross between hockey and lacrosse and was once used to help Celtic warriors learn the skills needed in battle. Shinty is played by a team of twelve, outdoors on a grass pitch with a caman, a long, wooden, curved stick with two slanted faces. The ball is slightly smaller than a tennis ball and made of cork, covered with a leather skin. The aim is to play

SHUTTERSTOCK/GWOEII

the ball into a 'hail' or goal at the end of the pitch.

Shinty was traditionally played through the winter months, and on New Year's Day villages would gather to play the game with no limit to the number in the teams. In the Isle of Uist stalks of seaweed were used as camans due to the lack of trees. Shinty is one of the forerunners of ice hockey and in the 1800s, Scottish immigrants to Nova Scotia played a game on ice. Edinburgh University Shinty Club was formed in 1891 and is one of the oldest clubs in Scotland.

GOLF

AN AULD SCOTTISH GAME

The game of **'gowf'** was so popular in Scotland that an Act of Parliament was passed in 1457 to forbid the playing of gowf on Sundays as there was concern that too much time was being spent playing golf and not enough on archery practice!

A ROYAL GAME

KING JAMES IV OF SCOTLAND *(1473–1513)* bought golf clubs from St Andrews Golf Club in 1506.

MARY QUEEN OF SCOTS *(1542–87)* was said to be playing golf at Seton House in Musselburgh in 1567, just a few days after the murder of her husband, Lord Darnley.

Mary, Queen of Scots (1542-1587) Engraved by T.W. Hunt and published in History of England, United Kingdom, 1845 SHUTTERSTOCK/GEORGIOS KOLLIDAS

St Andrews Links SHUTTERSTOCK/JEAN MORRISON

KING JAMES VI *(1566–1625)* played golf at Musselburgh before travelling south to be crowned King James I of England in 1603.

THE GOLF BALL

The Robertson family were famous for making 'featherie' golf balls in St Andrews for generations. In the 1840s, a new, more durable, gutta-percha golf ball, known as a 'gutty', was made from the dried sap of the Malaysian sapodilla tree. Although Allan Robertson was not keen on these new balls at first, he eventually changed to manufacturing them and the gutty transformed the game and led to the use of iron golf clubs.

The Royal Musselburgh Golf Club bought a hole cutter in 1829 and from then on all the holes at this club were 4.25 inches (10.79 cm) in diameter; this size was adopted as a standard in 1891.

LOCAL HISTORY

This is the time and this is the place!

THE NOR' LOCH AND DOUKIN' WITCHES

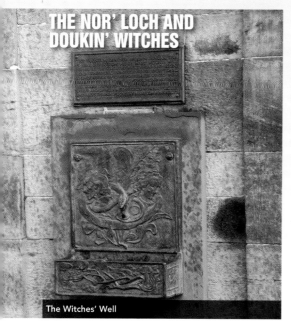

The Witches' Well

This fountain marks the spot where many witches were burned at the stake.

Edinburgh Castle sits proudly above the hustle and bustle of Scotland's capital city. The rock on which it stands is only one of Edinburgh's several volcanic hills. Originally there were many lochs but the only one that remains today is Duddingston in Holyroood Park. The site of Princes Street Gardens used to be the Nor' Loch, which was formed in the 15th century as King James III wished this forested valley to be flooded to strengthen the castle's defences, and about this time Edinburgh was made the capital of Scotland.

The Nor' Loch may have started out as an asset to the residents of Edinburgh as they could boat across it and skate upon it in the winter. However, this loch had other sinister uses such as the doukin' of witches. The suspected witch would have her thumbs and toes tied together and be douked on a special stool, into the loch, not once but twice. This was really a no win situation for if she sank and drowned she would be found innocent, but if she floated and survived she would be found guilty and burned at the stake on Castlehill. In the 16th century there were more burnings of witches here than anywhere else in Scotland. There is a plaque on the wall at Witches' Well, near the entrance to the Castle, in commemoration of over 300 women, accused of being witches, who were burnt at the stake.

However, over the years the Nor' Loch became a stinking cess-pool and obnoxious fumes and gases that rose from this sewer affected public health. Residents living in the wynds had hallucinations, caused by methane gas concentrating in the narrow closes. In 1759 a decision was taken to drain and fill the Nor' Loch and it was about this time that the building of the New Town commenced. The rubble from the building of the New Town was heaped up to create The Mound, where you will now find the Scottish National Gallery and the Royal Academy.

THE OLD TOWN

Originally, Edinburgh covered a small area around the Castle and in 1385, when the city was set alight by Richard II of England, it consisted of 400 houses. As Edinburgh grew as a trading centre, the High Street was the hub and the pattern of long wynds running back at right angles from this street was formed by gardens that were later built over. By the middle of the 15th century, 35,000 people

Paisley Close

Land, built in the 17th century and now owned by the National Trust for Scotland. These high buildings were prone to falling down and above Paisley Close, near John Knox House, is the carving of the face of a young boy and an inscription which reads, 'Heave awa chaps, I'm no' dead yet.' In 1861 a tenement collapsed killing 37 people, and just when the rescuers were about to give up they heard a voice crying out 'Heave awa chaps, I'm no' dead yet.' They set to work once more and saved the trapped boy. By the 1750s, Edinburgh was a booming trade centre and the Royal Exchange was built on top of several closes, including Mary King's Close, and you can book a guided tour of these underground closes. The building of the New Town attracted the wealthy merchants and professional classes and the Old Town fell into a state of decay with people living in cramped, unsanitary conditions.

lived in this area. Buildings grew taller due to the restrictions of space and cellars were excavated below street level. Some of the buildings on the Royal Mile exceeded ten storeys high, making them the first ever skyscrapers! A good example of a high-rise tenement in the Royal Mile is the six-storied Gladstone's

Georgian House in Charlotte Square SHUTTERSTOCK/BRENDAN HOWARD

THE NEW TOWN AND THE ENLIGHTENMENT

During the last half of the 18th century, thousands of new houses were built in an elegant layout of Georgian squares and courts on Barefoot's Parks, high ground to the north of the city. The architect, James Craig (1739–95), laid out the streets with uniformity, a dramatic change from the huddle of the Old Town. Craig may have been influenced by the layout of Richelieu in France, Inigo Jones' Covent Garden and Inverary in Argyle. Craig's plan showed George Street at the top of the natural ridge and the Lang Gait, now Princes Street, running parallel below and Queen Street parallel to the north. At one end of these three straight streets lies St Andrew Square and at the other end Charlotte Square, designed in 1791 by Robert Adam, who was influenced by the architecture he saw during his Grand Tour. An extension to the New Town was built in the 1820s and the buildings in Drummond Place, Royal Circus and Great King Street are less austere. Ainslie Place, Randolph Crescent and Moray Place, with its twelve-sided Roman Doric circus, was developed between 1822 and 1855 by the Earl of Moray.

Originally, town houses for the landed gentry were built along Princes Street but hotels, banks and shops soon began to appear. H.V.Morton says in his *In Search of Scotland (1929)*, 'Princes Street has been called the finest street in the kingdom. There are shops on one side only; the other side runs along a deep ravine, planted with gardens, above which rise the Castle Rock and the high roof-line of old Edinburgh.'

The building of the New Town coincides with a period from 1750 to 1800 called the Scottish Enlightenment, characterised by a flood of intellectual and scientific accomplishments. Adam Smith, David Hume. Alexander Nasmyth and Rabbie Burns all lived in Edinburgh for part of this period and this was also the time of 'Auld Reekie', as smoke from coal fires brought fog and smog to the city.

There were clubs where intense discussions took place on a daily basis and these included The Select Society and The Poker Club. The Enlightenment asserted the elementary importance of human reason combined with a rejection of any authority that could not be justified by reason. Some of the fields that rapidly advanced were philosophy, engineering, architecture, medicine and chemistry. It was in this atmosphere of a thirst for knowledge that Edinburgh printer, William Smellie, founded the *Encyclopaedia Britannica*, which was first published between 1768 and 1771.

BANKING, BEER AND BISCUITS

The fortunes of Edinburgh were built on banking and the law and the industries of beer, biscuits and publishing. The nearby Port of Leith gave access to world trading routes and this added to the city's prosperity.

Some of the Scots who influenced the banking system include John Napier (1550–1617) of Merchiston, who introduced the decimal point as well as logarithms, which he described in his book in 1614. William Paterson came up with the idea to create the Bank of England and he published

a paper with the proposal in 1691 and three years later the Bank of England was born. William Hogg was an Edinburgh merchant who had a thriving business but sometimes had cash-flow problems when customers were slow to pay. He went along to the Royal Bank of Scotland, who proposed to let him be overdrawn for a short time as they appreciated that the money would be paid. This was the very first overdraft in the world

Oak Aged Beer by Innis and Gunn on display on the Taste of Scotland shop in North Bridge

and it happened in Edinburgh in 1728. During the 19th and 20th centuries there were around thirty-five breweries in Edinburgh. William Younger started off brewing in Leith in 1749 and John Crabbie imported ginger from the Far East into the Port of Leith in 1801 to make Crabbie's Ginger Beer and Green Ginger Wine. William McEwan's Fountain Brewery produced beer here from 1856 until the 1990s. The Caledonian Brewery, established by Lorimer and Clark in 1869, continues brewing to this day with Deuchars IPA, popular with the author Ian Rankin and his character Inspector Rebus. The Edinburgh brewers, Innis and Gunn, discovered by accident the unique taste of oak-aged beer and one of the places you can buy this is the Taste of Scotland shop on North Bridge.

Robert McVitie and his father William opened a shop in Rose Street in 1830. Their baking proved to be so popular that it was not long before the family opened more shops. Charles Price joined the firm in 1875 and the large McVitie's and Price factory opened in 1888. Alexander Grant de Forres, who worked for the company, devised and produced the original Digestive Biscuit in 1892. It was over thirty years before chocolate digestives appeared on the market, around the same time as the Jaffa Cake. Eventually this company amalgamated with Macfarlane Lang and is now United Biscuits.

©SHUTTERSTOCK/ANTONY MCAULAY.

FISHWIVES AND HERRIN'

Leith has long been regarded as Edinburgh's port and it is where the Royal Yacht Britannia now lies. There was a shipbuilding industry here and it is where Edinburgh Zoo's first penguins arrived on whaling ships around the 1900s. The herring boats would also come in here and Carolina Oliphant (1766–1845), better known as Lady Nairne, wrote the song Caller Herrin', imitating the cries of the fishwives as they drum up business and ask for some sympathy for the fishermen who risk their lives to bring home the catch.

Wha'll buy my caller herrin'?
They're bonnie fish and halesome farin';
Wha'll buy my caller herrin'?
New drawn frae the Forth
When ye were sleepin' on your pillows,
Dreamed ye ought o' our puir fellows
Darkling as they faced the billows,
A' to fill our woven willows?

MONS MEG

Mons Meg is a medieval bombard, an early form of cannon, that was given to King James II by Duke Philip of Burgundy in 1454. This gun was capable of firing a 150kg cannonball for up to two miles. She was fired ceremoniously in 1558 when Mary, Queen of Scots married the French Dauphin. In 1680s her barrel burst and she lay unused at Edinburgh Castle until in 1754 she was taken to the Tower of London along with other Scottish weapons. Sir Walter Scott was

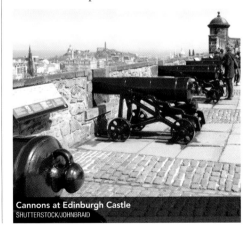

Cannons at Edinburgh Castle
SHUTTERSTOCK/JOHNBRAID

Edinburgh Castle SHUTTERSTOCK/CLAUDIO DIVIZIA

instrumental in having Mons Meg returned in 1829 and placed outside St Margaret's Chapel in Edinburgh Castle, where she can be seen today. The other famous gun at Edinburgh Castle is the booming One O'Clock Gun that roars out over the city every day except Sunday. This tradition dates back to the 1860s when the gun was fired at one o'clock to coincide with the time-ball dropping at the Nelson Monument so that ships in the Firth of Forth could set their maritime clocks.

The Nelson Monument, Calton Hill
SHUTTERSTOCK/HECTOR RUIZ VILLAR

The One O' Clock Gun at Edinburgh Castle
SHUTTERSTOCK/M R

FAMOUS LOCALS

SIR CHRIS HOY MBE

Sir Chris Hoy arriving for the Emeralds and Ivy Ball, London
SHUTTERSTOCK/FEATUREFLASH

is an Edinburgh lad and Olympic hero who was inspired to take to two wheels after watching the film, *E.T. The Extra-Terrestrial* when he was only six years old. Chris was brought up in Corstorphine and educated at George Watson's College followed by the University of St Andrews and then Edinburgh University. He raced BMX bikes and by the time he was fourteen years old, was ranked second in Britain and ninth in the world. Chris joined the City of Edinburgh Racing Club in 1994 and focused on track cycling, winning the World Cycling Championship several times. This Olympic champion has won a total of seven medals including three gold medals at the Beijing Olympics in 2008.

IRVINE WELSH

Irvine Welsh arriving for the premier of 'Filth'
SHUTTERSTOCK/FEATUREFLASH

was born in Edinburgh in 1958 and lived in a tenement in Leith before moving to West Pilton and then to Muirhouse. In 1978, he moved to London but eventually returned to Edinburgh and went on to study at Heriot Watt University. His first novel, *Trainspotting*, was published in 1993 and the film adaptation was released in 1996. Welsh appeared in the film as Mikey Forrester. The prequel, *Skagboys*, is set in Leith in the 1980s and introduces the *Trainspotting* characters. *Ecstasy*, a collection of short stories, went straight to number one on the Sunday Times best-sellers list as did his novel *Filth*, which was made into a film in 2013. Written in his native dialect, his books give a brutal view of Edinburgh life.

DAVID WILKIE MBE

Commonwealth Games Edinburgh 1970
SHUTTERSTOCK/FEATUREFLASH

was a student at Daniel Stewart's College in Edinburgh and a member of the Warrender Baths Club. Here he developed his breaststroke, breaking the British record for the 200 metres in 1970 and winning a bronze medal at the Edinburgh Commonwealth Games. He went on to win silver at the 1972 Munich Olympics and the World Championship in 1973. In 1974, he won two golds and a silver at the New Zealand Commonwealth Games. At the 1976 Olympics in Montreal, he won a gold medal in the 200 metres breaststroke and set a world-record time that was not beaten for eight years. He is said to be the first swimmer to wear a head-cap and goggles to improve his performance.

SIR ARTHUR CONAN DOYLE (1859–1930)

was born at 11 Picardy Place in Edinburgh and in 1867 his family lived at 3 Sciennes Place. After studying medicine at the University of Edinburgh, he worked as a doctor on the *Hope of Peterhead*, a Greenland whaling ship, in 1880 and on the *SS Mayumba* in 1881. Back on dry land, he practised medicine in Plymouth and then in Southsea. While waiting for patients he wrote stories and his first novel, *A Study in Scarlet*, which introduced the characters of Dr Watson and Sherlock Holmes, receiving good reviews from *The Scotsman* and *The Glasgow Herald* newspapers. Holmes was partially modelled on his teacher at Edinburgh University, Dr Joseph Bell. There is a statue of Sherlock Holmes in Picardy Place.

ALEXANDER GRAHAM BELL (1847–1922) was born at 14 South Charlotte Street, Edinburgh, making Edinburgh the home of the telephone. He was educated at James Maclaren's Hamilton Place Academy, the Royal High School in Calton Hill and the University of Edinburgh. His works and studies in teaching deaf people continued in London and in America, where he became a naturalised citizen in 1874. Working with his assistant Thomas A. Watson, Bell transmitted speech sounds using his membrane diaphragm transmitter in June 1875. A year later, after some improvements, they transmitted intelligible speech over wires. In 1880, Bell moved on to developing the photophone. It was no use for selfies but it enabled speech signals to be transmitted using a light beam powered by a selenium cell.

SIR WALTER SCOTT (1771–1832), born in College Wynd, Edinburgh, attended the Royal High School and Edinburgh University and became an advocate and a judge. When his first poems were published they were very popular with the public. He published his first novel, *Waverley*, a tale of the 1745 Jacobite Rising, anonymously and continued to write more historical novels as the 'Author

Statue of Sir Walter Scott

of *Waverley*'. When it became known that he was the author of these well-liked books, Jane Austen declared: 'Walter Scott has no business to write novels, especially good ones – It is not fair – He has fame and fortune enough as a poet…'. The Scott Monument in Edinburgh dominates Princes Street and Edinburgh's Railway Station is named after his *Waverley* novels.

SOPHIA JEX-BLAKE (1840–1912) studied medicine in specially arranged classes at Edinburgh University as female students were not allowed to attend lectures with the male students.

The Surgeons Hall Riot was instigated to prevent female students attending their exams and the University denied them their degrees. Sophia campaigned to have the law changed so that medical examination boards were forced to treat female students equally. Sophia qualified as a medical doctor in Berne.

In 1883 she set up a medical practice in Bruntsfield Lodge, which eventually became the Edinburgh Hospital for Women and Children and then the Bruntsfield Hospital, with an outpatient clinic and a dispensary for impoverished women. In 1886, she set up the Edinburgh School of Medicine for Women and the first woman to graduate was Jessie Chrystal MacMillan, who went on to become a barrister and a suffragette.

DAME MURIEL SPARK (1918–2006), poet and author, was born at 160 Bruntsfield Place in Edinburgh. She attended the James Gillespie's High School for Girls where she was encouraged by her teacher Christina Kay to become a writer. It was Christina who inspired the character of Miss Jean Brodie in Muriel's novel *The Prime of Miss Jean Brodie*, published in 1961. The novel is set in Edinburgh in the 1930s and Miss Brodie is determined to give six, ten-year-old girls a wide education so she includes lessons about love, travel, art history and fascism. The play became a hit in London's West End and New York's Broadway.

The film, directed by Ronald Neame in 1996, won actress Maggie Smith an Oscar. A plaque outside the James Gillespie School where Muriel Spark was educated and inspired to write her most famous work.

James Gillespie's
High School for Girls